Wear a Mask!
Oxford Pandemic Portraits

Martin Stott

T0352919

Signal

For Sue

First published in 2021 by
Signal Books Limited
36 Minster Road
Oxford OX4 1LY
www.signalbooks.co.uk

Photographs © Martin Stott, 2021
Foreword © Trisha Greenhalgh
End text © Patricia Baker-Cassidy

The right of Martin Stott to be identified as the author of this work has been asserted
by him in accordance with the Copyright, Design and Patents Act, 1988.

All rights reserved. The whole of this work, including all text and illustrations, is protected by copyright.
No parts of this work may be loaded, stored, manipulated, reproduced or transmitted in any form or by any
means, electronic or mechanical, including photocopying and recording, or by any information, storage and
retrieval system without prior written permission from the publisher, on behalf of the copyright owner.

A catalogue record for this book is available from the British Library

ISBN 978-1-8384630-2-1 Paper

Design and production: Ian Nixon
Editing and sequencing: Patricia Baker-Cassidy
Printed in Poland by Opolgraf

Signal

"There is one thing the photograph must contain, the humanity of the moment."

Robert Frank

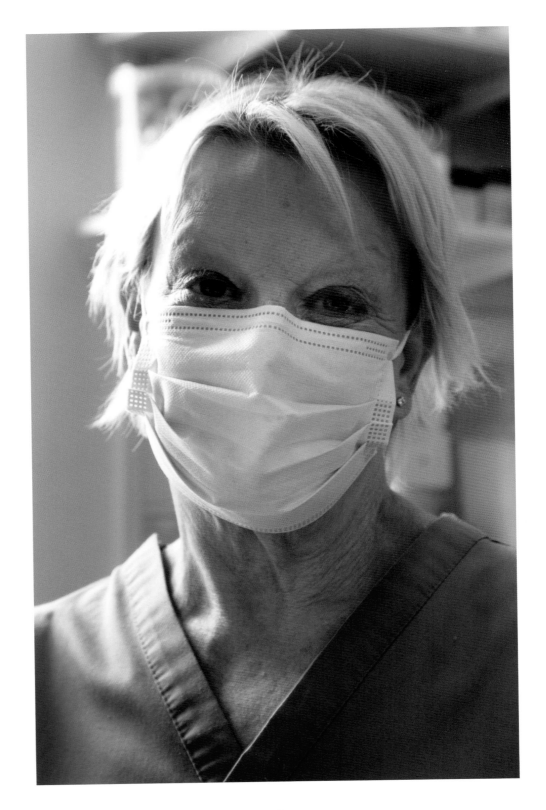

Foreword

Few topics in recent memory have generated as much emotional heat as the masking of ordinary citizens. Most Asian countries introduced masking policies within days of the first Covid-19 case. Most Western ones waited a hundred days or more. The UK took 167 days. This delay proved catastrophic because the mathematics of pandemics are such that cases double and then quadruple and then octuple within days, soon turning a handful of cases into thousands.

Scientists advising the World Health Organisation pointed out that no randomised controlled trial had yet demonstrated the efficacy of wearing masks. The fact that Thailand and Vietnam had few or no deaths from Covid-19 while the UK and USA had tens of thousands could not be attributed to masking, they said, because there were other "confounding variables" such as lockdown. Possible mask-induced harms, these scientists said, included "risk compensation" (if you're wearing a mask, you may ignore physical distancing or fail to wash your hands), self-contamination (adjusting the mask could transfer germs to your face) and psychological trauma.

Libertarians claimed that masks are ineffective and reduce blood oxygen levels, weaken the immune system and trigger viral infections that lie dormant in the body. They are also, allegedly, an attempt by government to control citizens and are therefore immoral.

These various claims did not hold water. Evidence from natural experiments that masks do work to prevent transmission is extremely strong. The harms of putting a piece of cloth over the face when going shopping or travelling on a bus are minimal, with some important exceptions such as people with claustrophobia or those who rely on lip-reading. Risk compensation does not occur. Indeed, people who mask are more likely to adhere to physical distancing and handwashing advice, and masked people touch their faces less frequently than unmasked ones. Self-contamination has never been demonstrated.

In an unprecedented public health emergency, and given the scientifically plausible arguments that masking *might* work, there is, therefore, a strong moral case for following the precautionary principle – masking "just in case" – without waiting for the so-called "gold standard" randomised controlled trial.

Zeynep Tufekci has argued (*The Atlantic*, 28 April 2021) that we wear masks for three reasons: to protect others from catching our germs, to protect ourselves from other people's germs, and to set social standards and norms appropriate for a pandemic. This book captures, for one English city in 2020, how people enacted new social standards and made their personal contribution to "normalising" the home-made or, in some cases, expensively purchased, face mask.

As the striking diversity of photographs illustrates, the mask is not merely a medical barrier to contagion. It is also a symbol of social solidarity; my mask protects you; yours protects me, and a powerful declaration of identity - my mask marks me out as responsible, safe and altruistic, but also as smart or casual, fashionable or drab, old or young.

To paraphrase Michelle Obama, and to counter the claims of some libertarians, masking policies have not changed who we are: they have helped to *reveal* who we are.

Trisha Greenhalgh

Introduction

This book comes out of the Covid-19 lockdown. It records a year, from 1 May 2020 to 30 April 2021, during that lockdown. The focus is on Oxford because I live in Oxford and under lockdown rules it was necessary to "stay local". The constraints of lockdown regulations provided an opportunity; the book documents my experience of lockdown both in terms of locality and uniqueness.

I conceived it as a social history. Mask wearing is not something that was widely done in the UK before the outbreak of the Covid pandemic in March 2020. It is, hopefully, an historical moment we will look back on remember and marvel at the strangeness of it all. Wearing a mask is an individual expression of collective solidarity. Wearing one probably won't stop you from contracting Covid, but if you carry the virus it will considerably reduce the chances of others catching it from you, as the virus is transmitted through aerosols when you breathe out. It is an expression of humanity at its best.

The images mainly consist of portraits of people wearing masks going about their daily life outdoors, and reflects their experience of and response to the constraints of lockdown. This is important because they record absence as well as presence. Quite a few people were shielding on government advice or because they felt that it was unsafe to be out in public. They are not recorded. Many of them were older, more vulnerable, or poorer members of the community. Nonetheless the images reflect and celebrate the diversity of the people of Oxford. I have chosen not to name any of them because mask wearing was part of a *collective* effort to tackle the spread of the virus. The response of NHS staff and volunteers delivering vaccines is also recorded, as is the specific Oxford dimension, the Oxford AstraZeneca vaccine itself, developed and manufactured in the city.

I try to document people's responses to the circumstances they found themselves in and in all weathers; queuing at shops or markets for essential food shopping while non-essential shops were closed; waiting at hubs such as bus stops or the rail station when travel restrictions were eased but mask wearing was compulsory; queuing for their vaccination from the start of 2021; or engaged in some of the significant political movements that marked the year, including Black Lives Matter (page 35), Extinction Rebellion (page 33) and protests against the Policing Bill. Their concerns with breathing, "I can't breathe" (BLM), ''Pause and Breathe" (XR) highlighting the impact racial injustice, and of poor air quality due to fossil fuel burning, echoed in the experiences of Covid sufferers.

These responses could be fearful, especially at first, with highly elaborate and technical masks or "double masking"; utilitarian – the ubiquitous throw away light blue or black surgical-style masks; fashion conscious; expressions of identity or "tribal" affiliation; playful, beautiful, or combined with hats, scarves and dark glasses, to create acts of disguise. They also reflect multiple identities, like the young man from East Timor in his Union Jack mask (page 43). The images also reflect the artistic response these colours, designs, clothing combinations, identities and contexts, evoked in me as a photographer.

For a photographer interested in documenting people, masks also disrupt the most common relationship between photographer and subject, the "smile please" or "say cheese" dynamic. Behind a mask the subject can be smiling or grave, but the visual signals are, largely, absent.

These photographs are therefore a record of this collective and individual response to an event and set of specific personal circumstances that I and the subjects experienced over a dramatic, unprecedented and, for many, tragic year.

Martin Stott

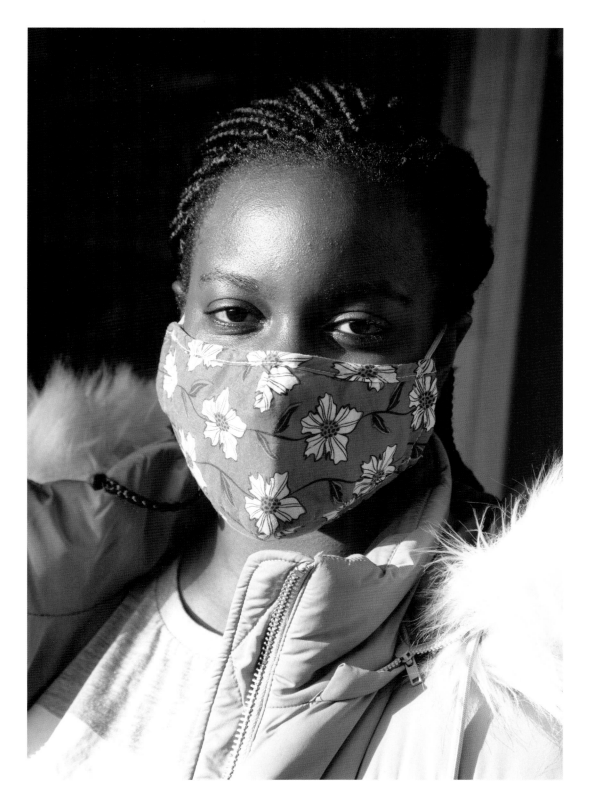

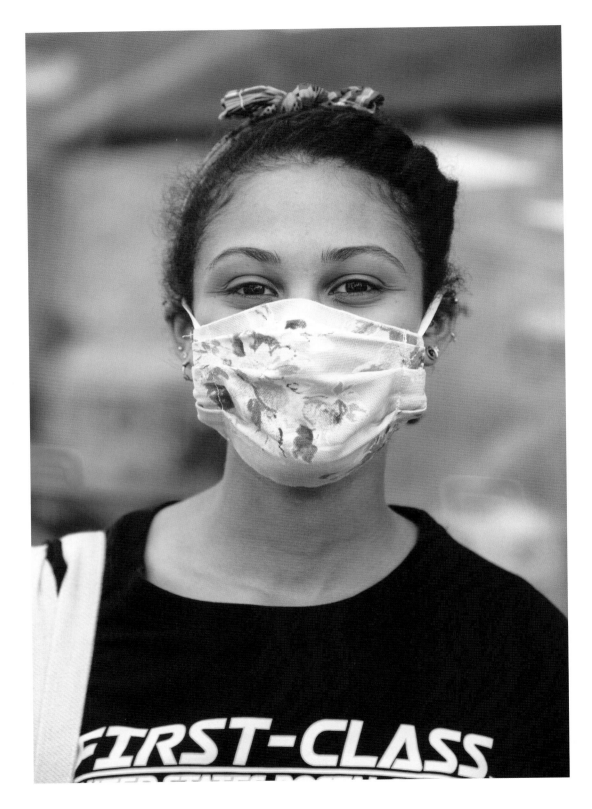

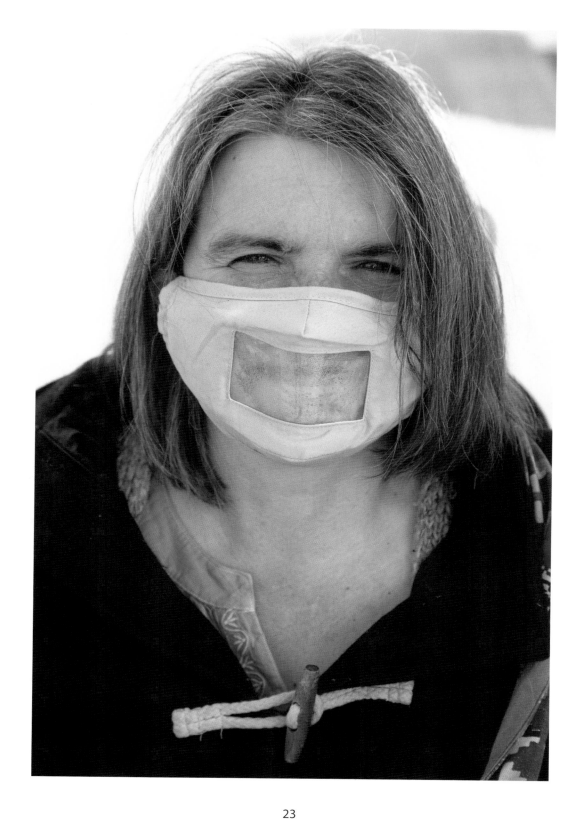

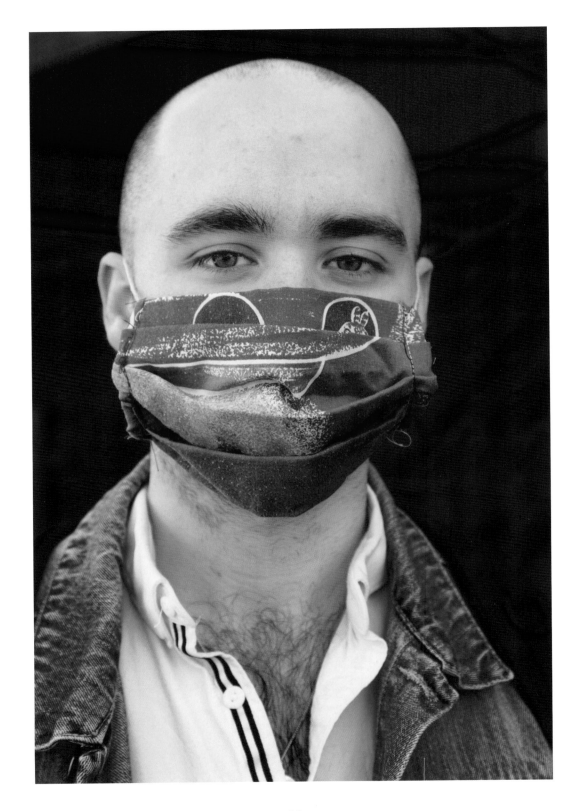

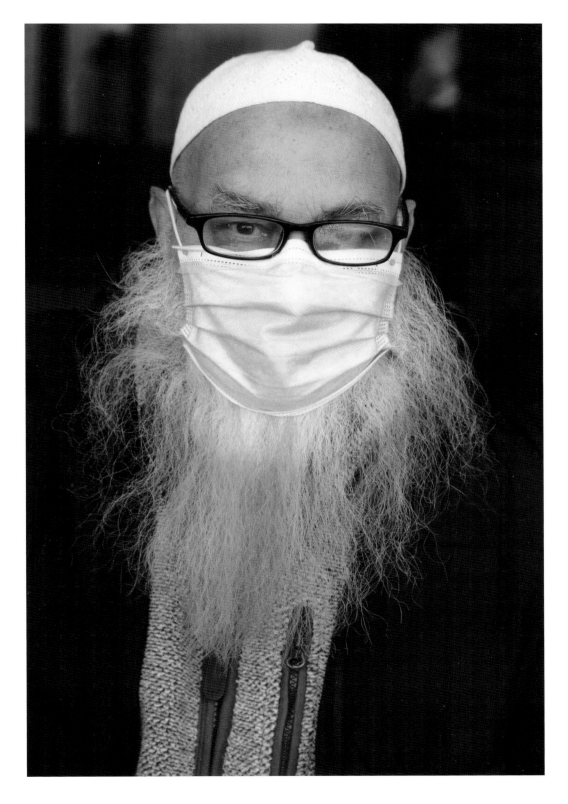

Wear a mask! Oxford pandemic portraits

In 2020 overnight, the constraint of access so often experienced by street photographers became constraints we all experienced. Our daily lives, our routines, our streets, even our reflections in shop windows, became de-familiarised. Suddenly we were plunged into uncertainty.

Martin Stott, circumscribed as we all were, "stayed home", taking exercise within the narrow permissions of the first lockdown. And, taking his camera... As he said himself: "I made this essay almost accidentally. It was some weeks before I realised what I was doing." The accidental nature of the origin of this project reflects on a smaller scale, the improvisational nature of early official responses to the unprecedented pandemic.

Wandering his local streets, Stott took portraits of friends, neighbours, strangers. Hidden by masks, yet refusing to be hidden, he shows many, many people disinclined to vanish in the face of an invisible threat. Perhaps the improvised and jokey approach demonstrated by some of the mask-wearers is a typically British response, that touching mix of ramshackle and defiant, reminding us of Dad's Army. Certainly, some of the masks portrayed carry overtones of war...

The overcast national mood

The shifting moods of lockdown are captured in these photographs. We see the nervous anxiety that we all felt, sometimes expressed through exaggerated masks. Floral and comedic masks suggest the resilience that was more than a purely local experience. The light changes. We recall that first glorious spring, but portraits in overcast dull light remind us of the overcast national mood, as the struggle dragged on, and the virus toll mounted.

Stott has adopted a uniform format for the portraits. He keeps same distance, the same lens, and more or less the same framing, which makes the subject matter more important than the photographic method. These chosen constraints of the format - the tightly cropped portraits, almost always single people - echo the constraints of daily life under lockdowns... the distancing, the isolation.

Stott employs no quirky photographic devices, nothing to draw attention to the photographic method such as unusual angles, or strongly directional lighting. Documenting the subject, with care and respect, remains his central concern. Just as the need to mask did not impose uniformity and obliterate individual personality, so the uniformity of Stott's approach does not negate individuality. And as we gaze on these faces from the streets of Oxford, we are made to wonder about the "masks" of presentation in pre-pandemic days. Here, faces are half hidden, make-up barely present, even gender sometimes uncertain... yet intense individuality shines out.

A focal point of the fightback

Like the rest of the country, Oxford became a masked city. But Oxford also became a focal point of the fightback. Teams that had worked on the Sars virus revisited research they had mothballed, as a platform to launch an extraordinary and unprecedented effort of vaccine engineering, responding to live data, and to an alarming physical and social danger.

Oxford did not emerge unscathed. As elsewhere, there were illness and deaths, financial hardship and of course huge pressures on the NHS in a city which, because it is a beacon for health care, experienced stress commensurately. And in the dark of winter, from the heroic efforts of the Oxford research teams, the sparks of hope emerged. This city, this country, are forever grateful.

As Martin Stott's portraits show, through the communal duty of mask-wearing there emerges a sense of a community character: both compliant and subversive, anxious and sarcastic, blackly humorous and cheerfully determined.

The uncertainties expressed in these masked faces remain. In ten years' time will mask-wearing be so routine that readers might wonder why anyone should bother to record it, or will these photographs be viewed as a valuable document of an aberrant but vanished point in our shared histories?

Patricia Baker-Cassidy

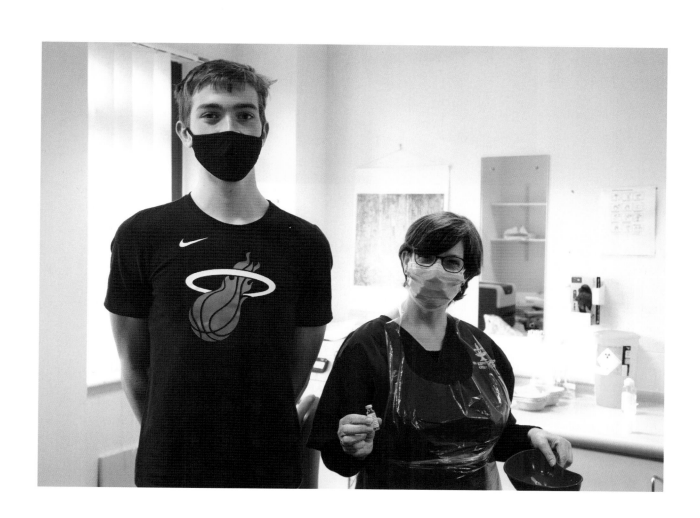

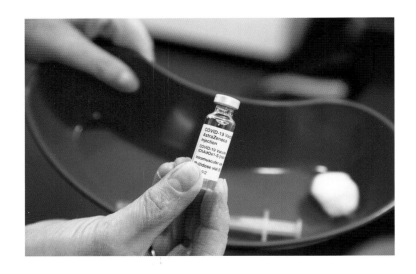

Acknowledgements

I am grateful for the support and encouragement of members of the Oxford Photographers Group, in particular Wendy Aldiss, Patricia Baker-Cassidy, Paul Freestone, Kazem Hakimi and Paddy Summerfield. The participants on the Martin Parr Foundation photography course in June 2019, were a source of inspiration and insight. The continuing engagement through our 'Tenby togs' WhatsApp group has been a joy. Keith Barnes of the Oxford Photographer's Workshop has, over almost 40 years, taught me a huge amount about photography, and been a constant source of encouragement and critical support. Helen Ganly has helped me develop the eye of a visual artist as well as being a good friend. Martin Parr, David Hurn and Jon McCall have all been appropriately critical as well as introducing me to new perspectives and photographers.

I would like to thank all my subjects who agreed to be photographed for this project, whether they appear in the book or not. And to all the NHS vaccination staff and volunteers who agreed to be photographed while I was acting as a vaccination volunteer.